Magellan the Magical

Or How Dreams Become Real

By Krystal M. Harris

Illustrated by Lorinda Tomko

Published in the United States in 2022 by Krystal Muse Les Enfants, an imprint of Krystal Muse Publishing, a division of Krystal Muse Incorporated, California.

Illustrations by Lorinda Tomko with Codex Art and Apparel
Book design and formatting by Bainton House Books

Library of Congress Control Number: 2022907997

ISBN: 979-8-9858998-2-5

Krystal Muse Les Enfants books may be available for special discounts for educational institutions and libraries. For details, contact publishing@krystalmuseinc.com

KRYSTAL MUSE
Incorporated

This book is dedicated to you, dear reader.

Whether young or old, the child in you has beautiful dreams that are meant to unfold. You are here for a reason and your special mark upon this world is meant to be realized. May you go forth with the knowledge that thoughts become things, and magic does indeed exist.

It is always there for you, waiting to help make your dreams... real.

PROLOGUE

Once upon a time, in a small country town, there lived an eight-year-old boy named Kodi. He was an ordinary child with an extraordinary imagination. Kodi dreamed big, much like any child his age... much like you.

Kodi's dreams visited him every night, but were quickly forgotten when he woke up the next day. However, Kodi's life changed forever when he learned that the magic of his dreams really did exist, and that it started with a simple thought.

This is the story of how Kodi met Magellan and learned how to make his magnificent dreams real.

CHAPTER ONE

Kodi was smart, curious, playful, and, most of all, loved. He lived in a beautiful brick house with his mother and his father. Although Kodi was an only child, he found ways to entertain himself.

In the hot summer months, Kodi would travel down to the lake's edge. He would marvel at his reflection in the glassy water, and he would play and skip along the shoreline. He would pick flowers for his mother, and fashion them into beautiful crowns fit for a queen.

Kodi would take a long rope and tie it around the branches of the strong oak tree near the lake. He would hold on to one end and count to three...

...and then he would swing from the tree into glorious cannonballs, splashing wildly and happily into the crisp, cool waters.

In the spring, Kodi would climb the apple tree in front of his house to pick the ripening fruit. The apples from this tree, his father once told him, were grown with a special ingredient: love. And it showed, because every apple from Kodi's tree had a heart shape on its shiny surface. Kodi liked to help others, so he would take the heart-marked apples and give them to the merchants at the local farmer's market to sell.

Fall was Kodi's favorite time of year. During this season, the leaves began to burst with color. Beautiful hues of orange, red, and yellow adorned every tree that his young eyes could see. The richness of the color filled Kodi's heart with warmth, and it never failed to give him inspiration.

Kodi longed to be like the birds above, so free and powerful, soaring up in the sky. So when the leaves fell from the trees and piled up on the ground, he would gather them into huge bunches and tie them to sticks with some rope. He would fashion wings as big as an eagle's, slide them over his shoulders, and then...

...he would try to fly.

When the cold wind of winter arrived, Kodi would run outside full of glee, bundled from head to toe in mittens, scarves, and a puffy jacket. Kodi would lie down in the heavy snow, waving his arms and legs to make divine snow angels.

And then he would have thrilling snowball fights...

...alone.

It was not long before Kodi realized just how alone he really was. Even in this land of wonder, he longed for a true friend. The children at school were not Kodi's friends. They teased him and called him names because he was born with a peculiar mark upon his face.

"Your birthmark," his mother explained, "is there to remind you how special you are. You are the only person with this mark, and that means you are the only one who looks like you, and thinks like you, and most importantly, dreams big like you. You, my dear son, are unique."

But Kodi did not feel unique, and he did not think that there was anything special about him or his dreams. At home, he was happy, but out there in the world, Kodi was often very sad.

All of that changed one fateful day, as Kodi was walking home from school. There were three bullies who always seemed to pick on Kodi: Wally, Rex, and Sal. Every day these bullies did something to hurt poor Kodi's feelings. They made fun of his birthmark, they took his lunch, and they intimidated him any chance they could get. This day was no exception.

As Kodi walked the long path home, he heard Rex, Wally, and Sal behind him.

"Get him!" shouted Rex.

Rex began to chase after Kodi, and the other two bullies followed close behind. Kodi ran as fast as he could to escape, but the bullies chased him down the street... over the hill... and into the park, where they finally had him cornered.

"Give it here!" Wally yelled, as he ripped Kodi's backpack from him.

"There's nothing good in here," Sal chimed in, as he rummaged through the sparse bag.

"What about his shoes?" Rex sneered mischievously, eyeing Kodi's winter boots. Kodi shivered with fear as the bullies began inching closer to him.

"Leave that boy alone!" cried a voice from across the park.

The voice came from an old woman who was standing near the swings. She had kind eyes and gray hair, and her arms were full of groceries. As she screamed at the bullies, one of the bags fell from her arms, and all the fresh fruit she had bought from the farmer's market spilled out into the snow. The bullies let go of Kodi's bag and walked over to the old woman. She snarled at them.

"That's okay," said Rex. "He's not worth it anyway."

Rex grabbed an apple from the woman's fallen bag and took a bite before walking away. As the bullies trudged away, Kodi began to help the old woman with her bags. He noticed that the apples she had all bore a heart-shaped symbol, just like the ones he would pick from his tree.

"We have a tree with apples just like this!" Kodi exclaimed.

The old woman looked at Kodi with smiling eyes. "I always look forward to these apples. Not only are they the sweetest I've ever tasted, the hearts on their skin remind me to be kind and to always seek joy and love. Every time I go to the market," she continued, "I hope that they are there, and I am always grateful when they are."

Kodi smiled, thinking about what his father told him about the apples and their secret recipe. Then his brow furrowed as he watched Wally, Rex, and Sal fade into the distance.

"Sorry about those guys," Kodi remarked. "They always do this."

"Are they your friends?" she asked.

"No," Kodi replied. "I don't have any friends."

"Well," the old woman said calmly, "that shouldn't be."

She reached into her bohemian purse and pulled out a stuffed toy wolf with bright blue eyes, beautiful gray fur, and a white stripe down its back.

"Take this," she said as she handed the toy to Kodi. "His name is Magellan. I think he would love to be your friend."

"Thank you!" Kodi said as he took Magellan and embraced him.

"No," whispered the old woman. "Thank you."

Kodi examined Magellan's fur and noticed that he had a peculiar star-shaped mark on his forehead. Kodi touched his own birthmark curiously. When he looked back up, the old woman had disappeared.

CHAPTER TWO

Kodi took Magellan everywhere. He stuffed him inside of his backpack on his walks to school, taught him tricks, and read bedtime stories with him. Thanks to that old woman, Kodi now had someone to play with... and play he did.

At school, Wally, Rex, and Sal continued to bully Kodi. But now that he had Magellan, he did not mind as much. He was too busy telling Magellan all of his hopes, dreams, and secrets. He was truly happy, and even though Magellan was just a toy, he felt real to Kodi, like the friend he had always longed for. Kodi's constant sadness was replaced with a new feeling: joy.

As the months passed, Kodi and Magellan played from sunup to sundown. They played so much together that Magellan's gray fur became matted and worn. He hardly looked like a toy that a child would want, let alone cherish. However, none of that mattered to Kodi, for Kodi had learned that true friends are there for you in the happy times and in the sad times. It did not matter what he looked like now. What mattered was that Magellan was always there for Kodi, and Kodi was always there for Magellan.

One night, Kodi held Magellan in his arms and hugged him tight. "You are my best friend, Magellan," he whispered as he slowly fell asleep. "I love you." And as he lay sleeping, he dreamed the most marvelous dream...

Kodi dreamed that he was flying a majestic plane in the fall-colored sky. He flew over a bountiful apple orchard. There were miles and miles of trees, as far as the eye could see. Each tree was filled to the brim with heart-marked apples. He landed his plane in a clearing and stepped out. Beautiful rust-colored trees and golden grass greeted him. He marveled at the sight. Then something amazing happened.

In the distance, a lone wolf began walking toward him. No, not just any wolf... it was Magellan. But here, in this dream, he was not worn and matted at all. He was not even a toy. He was a strong and powerful, living and breathing wolf, with glowing blue eyes. The star symbol on his head shone as bright as his silver coat, and the white stripe on his back seemed to sparkle with light.

"Magellan?" Kodi questioned, with a shocked and cracking voice. "Is that you?"

"Yes, Kodi. It is I, your best friend, Magellan."

"How are you here... in my dream?" Kodi asked.

"You invited me. When you told me how much you cared, you let me know that I could now show you what I have wanted to show you since I first met you," Magellan replied.

"What is it?" Kodi asked, his curiosity growing.

"Come with me," Magellan said as they began walking through the orchard.

"Look around you," Magellan said. "This is your dream. It's beautiful, isn't it?"

"Yes!" Kodi exclaimed. "I flew a plane, Magellan, and I saw so many wonderful things! I think I want to do that again, and again, and again," Kodi shouted excitedly, waving his arms wildly and pretending to soar like an eagle. Then he stopped and looked at Magellan. "I mean, in real life," he said solemnly.

"That is what I wanted to show you, Kodi," Magellan said, his voice full of wisdom. "You can turn this dream into a reality."

"I can?" Kodi questioned. "How?"

"You can have anything you want, if you just ask for it in the right way," Magellan said.

"What is the right way?" Kodi questioned, scratching his head.

"Start by writing it down," Magellan answered. "For example, 'I want... to fly airplanes'," Magellan stated calmly.

"That's just a wish, Magellan. And this is just a dream," Kodi responded glumly.

"A dream, Kodi, is your heart's way of guiding you toward your purpose. If you want it, write it down."

"How will that help me?" Kodi argued.

"If you write your dreams down, I will go and get them for you." Kodi was puzzled.

Magellan walked further into the dreamscape, through the lush golden blades of grass, admiring the orange-tinted sky above. He sat down, watching the sun dip below the horizon.

"In this world, your dreams have no power," Magellan explained. "You must bring these wishes into the real world for me to be able to help. You must write them down."

"So, anything I want you will get for me, as long as I write it down?" Kodi asked, beginning to get excited.

"Anything good that your heart desires, I will get for you. But you must focus hard on what it is and then write, 'I want...'"

"To fly airplanes!" Kodi finished.

Magellan smiled, "That, and whatever else you want."

Kodi looked out into the distance for a moment, and then he turned to Magellan and asked, "Magellan, can I draw what I want? You know, like pictures, instead?"

"Of course you can, Kodi. In fact, I love pictures because they are usually very detailed. It makes it easier for me to see exactly what you want," Magellan responded.

"Wait... Will I see you in my dreams again?" Kodi asked.

"Yes... I'm always here for you," Magellan said, before he disappeared into the sunset.

When Kodi woke up, he began drawing all of the things he wanted. He drew a picture of a red mountain bike with a bright orange flame on it. He drew his family home with a new pool and a brand-new big tire swing in the backyard. He drew himself surrounded by lots of friends. And he drew the old woman who gave him Magellan. In his drawing, she was surrounded by the apple orchards from his dream. Kodi thought to himself, *Now she will never have to hope for them. They will always be right there, just like Magellan.* Finally, he drew himself flying a magnificent airplane.

Then he wrote, "I want" on all of his drawings.

It was not long until Kodi experienced the first bit of Magellan's magic. It happened on his birthday.

"Happy birthday, my sweet boy!" his mother squealed as Kodi came down for breakfast. Kodi sat down and ate a whole helping of his favorite meal: apple-filled pancakes.

"Ready for your birthday gift?" Kodi's father asked, before disappearing into the garage.

He returned and, to Kodi's astonishment, he rolled in a bright red mountain bike with an orange flame painted on it!

"Wow!" Kodi exclaimed. "It's exactly what I wanted! How did you know?"

"Something told us this one would be perfect for you," Kodi's mother explained.

"Thank you so much! I love you!" Kodi said as he hugged his parents in disbelief.

"We love you too, Kodi," they said as they hugged him back tightly.

Then he was off. He strapped Magellan to the handlebars, and the two of them rode the new bike until the streetlights came on.

CHAPTER THREE

That night, Kodi had another dream. This time he was surrounded by friends. The bullies who bothered him in real life were giving him high fives, and everyone seemed to love him. Kodi was so happy.

"Friends are an important part of life," he heard a voice say.

Kodi turned around to see Magellan inside his dream once again, in his true wolf form.

"But you must choose them wisely," Magellan added.

"You're my only friend, Magellan," Kodi said sadly. "This... this would never happen," Kodi said as he pointed to his dream.

"The world is full of friends, Kodi. Even those who look like your enemies could be your friends."

"I don't think so," Kodi replied. "Wally and the other bullies don't want to be my friends. They only want to hurt my feelings."

"Kodi, look at your dream now. Are they your friends here, in this dream world?"

"Yes," Kodi replied.

"Then they can be your friends in the real world, too. If you think it and then really believe it, it will come true, one way or another... like a magnet. But I do have to warn you," Magellan said. "That magnet works both ways. If you think unkind thoughts or you ask for something that doesn't belong to you, that magnet will bring you unkind things... things that are not for you."

Kodi paused and thought about this.

"I think I understand," he said. "I should only ask for what I want, and really believe that I will get it, and never ever ask for things that belong to someone else," Kodi repeated.

"Or unkind things," Magellan added.

Kodi looked at Magellan and thought for a moment. "Magellan! It was you, wasn't it? The bike?"

"Yes Kodi, it was you and me, together."

Kodi thought about Magellan's words before asking, "How?"

"It works in mysterious ways, Kodi. You had a dream, which meant your heart had a desire, and then you put it out into the real world. I then knew exactly what you wanted, and I started to look for it back home in the physical realm."

"But... how?" Kodi asked again.

Magellan smiled, sensing that Kodi wanted to know how the magic worked.

"I found an old man who owns a toy shop," Magellan continued. "He is someone who dreams of making children happy. So I inspired him to paint the exact bike you pictured."

"How did my parents find that man?" Kodi asked.

"I helped them," Magellan said. "The man was so excited to show off his latest creation. They, too, felt inspired and couldn't leave the store without that bike," Magellan explained.

"That is amazing," Kodi said, slowly understanding.

"Do you remember the first lesson?" Magellan asked curiously.

"Yes, write it down and say that I want it," Kodi responded.

"Yes, and what comes next?" Magellan inquired, the star on his head starting to glow with anticipation.

"Believe that I will get it, and be careful with my thoughts so I don't get unkind things."

"Very good, Kodi. Do this, and it will make all of the difference," Magellan responded, satisfied.

"Um... Magellan?" Kodi asked.

"Yes, Kodi?" Magellan replied.

"Can I ask for more?" Kodi questioned with pleading eyes.

"Always," Magellan said gently. "I'm always here for you," he reminded Kodi, and then he disappeared. Once again, Kodi woke up.

When he awoke, he got back to drawing. This time, he drew a huge house filled with friends, family, and love. He wrote "I want" on the photo, held it close to his heart, closed his eyes, and said, "I believe."

The next day at school, Kodi saw Wally and the other bullies at recess.

"Hey!" yelled Wally as he stomped toward Kodi.

Kodi remembered what Magellan said and, as Wally got closer, Kodi smiled the biggest smile ever and quickly said, "Wait!"

Wally stopped in his tracks.

Kodi rummaged through his backpack and pulled out one of the apples from his tree. He handed it to Wally.

"Here," he said. "I brought this for you. I actually brought enough for everyone," he continued as he grabbed more apples and handed them to Sal and Rex.

Wally, Rex, and Sal started to eat the apples and couldn't help but smile. The special ingredient of love was surely beginning to take effect.

"Wally, how are you today?" Kodi asked, surprising Wally.

"Huh?" Wally asked in confusion.

"I'm sorry, something told me that maybe no one had asked you that in a really long time. So... how are you, really?" Kodi repeated.

Wally scratched his head, then looked down at his shoes. Kodi was right. No one, not even Wally's own parents, had asked Wally how he was feeling, and he had been feeling very sad for months.

"Um... I guess I'm not doing too well. My dog passed away a few months ago. And I've been really sad about it," Wally admitted.

"I'm really sorry," Kodi said. "That must have been really hard."

"It was," Wally said as he took another bite of the sweet, crisp apple.

"What was your dog's name?" Kodi asked.

"Her name was Cookie Dough," Wally said sadly. "Thanks for asking."

"You're welcome," Kodi replied.

Then Kodi got an idea. "Hey Wally, did you get to say goodbye to Cookie Dough? I mean, properly say goodbye?"

"No. My parents just told me after they came back from the vet," Wally responded.

"Hmmm . . ." Kodi mumbled as he thought. "Meet me after school. I have a plan."

After school, Wally, Sal, and Rex met Kodi in the park.

Kodi gave each of them white flowers that he had picked from his mother's flower garden. Together, they said goodbye to Cookie Dough and honored her for all the joy that she had brought to Wally while she was with him.

"Kodi?" Wally said after a while. "I'm really sorry I was so mean to you."

"Thank you for saying that, Wally. You guys really hurt my feelings and you never even took the time to get to know me. So I never understood why you were so mean," Kodi said earnestly.

"Well, I do know one thing about you: You are kind, Kodi," Wally said patting Kodi on the back, "Maybe we can start over, if that's okay with you?"

Kodi smiled happily. "I would like that!" he exclaimed. Wally was so happy, and from that moment on, he never bullied Kodi again.

In fact, they became great friends because they both now felt understood, seen, and not alone.

As time moved on, Kodi became friends with many more people, always remembering that if he thought it and believed it, he could receive it.

CHAPTER FOUR

Kodi was beginning to grow up, and two years had passed since that moment with Wally, Rex, and Sal. They were a great group of friends now, and Kodi had outgrown playing with a stuffed animal. He stopped receiving signs of Magellan's magic, and he had not seen him in his dreams for some time. That was because he was living his dream, with his bike and his new friends.

Kodi was ten years old by then, and he started to believe that maybe Magellan was not really magical at all. Maybe he was just an imaginary friend... a child's plaything. He was growing up and did not have time to believe in imaginary friends, or even to play with toys.

But later that year, Kodi's world came crashing down, and that was when he needed his truest friend the most. Kodi's mother and father sat him down and told them that they were going to be separating and moving into different houses. Kodi didn't understand, because he always felt that their family was a happy one. He started to feel the saddest he had ever felt. He felt like it was his fault. Kodi's father moved to the next town over, and his mother had to move into a smaller house just on the edge of town. That meant that Kodi had to change schools. Once again, Kodi was very sad.

Kodi sat in his brand new house surrounded by moving boxes, and he began crying. Then, he saw the box labeled "Kodi's Things".

It was only then that he remembered his old, faithful friend, Magellan. *Would he still remember me?* Kodi thought.

Kodi wanted to see if maybe, just maybe, Magellan had a little bit of magic left in him. So he scooped him out of the box and hugged him tight.

"I'm very scared, I didn't want to move. I miss my friends and my school. I miss my old house and my apple trees. I miss my family the way it used to be. I'm all alone again," Kodi whispered as he cried into Magellan's matted coat.

"Are you still my best friend?" Kodi asked. Then a peaceful sleep began to wash over him. As he lay there in the empty room, hugging Magellan and breathing softly, he began to dream.

This time, Kodi dreamed of a desert, where he was all alone.

"I will always be your friend," a familiar voice said.

Kodi turned around to see Magellan walking through the sand. "Magellan! It's really you!" Kodi exclaimed as he hugged the majestic wolf.

"Why are you so scared, Kodi?" Magellan asked.

"Everything is changing," Kodi said.

"Change can be good. Have you written things down? Have you been believing?" Magellan asked.

"I did, but I never got anything else that I asked for. You abandoned me," Kodi said angrily.

"Kodi, I will always be here. I am always working for you. Some things take time," Magellan said. "There is something else, too."

"What is it?" asked Kodi.

"You must always be thankful for everything you have. But it is even more powerful to be thankful for things that you want, as though you already have them."

"How can I be thankful for stuff I want but don't have?" Kodi asked.

"It's easy. Imagine that you have them already," Magellan explained. "When you think of what you want, think of how happy you will be when it comes to you. Then try to be that happy now... before you have it."

Kodi curled up his nose in frustration. "You already told me to be thankful for the things I don't have... now I have to be happy about it, too?" he asked, pouting.

"Yes," replied Magellan. "Think of it like a game of tug-of-war. If you write down something that you want and just leave it, then it is almost like you are tugging on the rope all by yourself. The fact is, you need help to win a game like that."

"Isn't that what you are for?" Kodi remarked.

"Yes, that is true. But I need help to win, too," Magellan stated.

"Happy thoughts and a thankful attitude are like two strong friends that we can add to our team. When the four of us pull together, it's much stronger. With that kind of strength, I can locate and return your dreams to you at the perfect time, just when you really need them. It's the secret recipe to getting everything you want," Magellan concluded.

"What was the first lesson I taught you?" Magellan asked, as usual.

"Write it down and say that I want it," Kodi responded,

"And the second?" Magellan pushed.

"Believe that I will get it, and be careful with my thoughts so I don't get unkind things," he said, remembering the lesson from long ago.

"And now what have you learned?"

"To be thankful even if I don't have it yet. I must also be happy," Kodi said, starting to feel better just thinking about happy thoughts.

"This is a very important rule, Kodi," said Magellan sternly. "But it works every time. Remember, I'm always here for you."

Magellan then disappeared, leaving Kodi alone with his happy and thankful thoughts.

When Kodi woke up, he saw Magellan tangled in the blanket next to him.

"Be thankful for the things I don't yet have, as though I already have them," Kodi said to himself as he got out of bed.

He went back to the moving box and looked inside. There he found his old drawings, and he pulled each and every one of them out. He stared for a moment, and then he began adding the secret recipe.

"And be happy," Kodi said, as he admired all of the dreams in front of him.

Then his eyes shifted to the drawing of the house with a tire swing and a pool. He sighed, longing for it to be true. He remembered his lessons and was filled with gratitude and happiness.

Chapter Five

The next morning, Kodi woke up to his mother calling him. "Kodi!" she shouted from the next room. "Come here, I want to show you something!"

Kodi got out of bed and walked over to his mother, who was waiting near the front door. She held his hand and led him outside. "Look!" she said with excitement. Kodi did look, and what he saw stopped him in his tracks. Outside of his mother's new home was a strong oak tree with a brand-new tire swing tied to its branch. Kodi hugged his mother and then jumped on for a ride.

The next week, Kodi went to his father's new house. When he walked into the backyard, he saw the most splendid sight: a huge pool! "No way!" Kodi exclaimed.

"Yes way!" replied his father, smiling from ear to ear.

The two of them quickly ran into the house, changed into swim clothes, and jumped into the pool. They decided to start a new tradition with just the two of them: a cannonball contest. Kodi won, of course. He had been practicing for years.

That night Kodi dreamed again. This time he dreamed of a green pasture, with a tree stump perfect for sitting on. Right next to the stump was Magellan.

"It worked, it worked!" Kodi shouted as he danced around.

"I told you... it always does," said Magellan.

"I didn't think I would get what I wanted like that, though. It's kind of sad. But I am still thankful," Kodi remarked.

"Kodi, your parents still love you no matter what. This wasn't your fault. They each had dreams of their own, and I had to help them find what they wanted. Just like I helped you."

"You helped my parents?" Kodi asked.

"I help anyone who asks it of me," Magellan responded.

"I am sorry I ever doubted you. You are the best thing that ever happened to me!"

"Kodi, you are the best thing that ever happened to me, too. When you believe in me and in what I can do, I also become thankful and happy."

Kodi hugged his friend once more.

"Do you remember your lessons now, Kodi?" Magellan asked.

"Yes," Kodi replied. "I must write it down, and say that I want it. I must believe that I will get it, and be careful with my thoughts so I don't get unkind things. I must be thankful even if I don't have it yet, and I must be happy," Kodi said, proud of himself.

"You make me very proud, Kodi," Magellan said warmly. Kodi watched as Magellan looked out over the dreamscape. He saw the glow of his fur. The white star on his head was glowing. Magellan looked powerful, but Kodi became sad.

"Magellan?" Kodi asked. "Back home, you're a stuffed animal. You are worn and dirty, and your stitching is loose. What will happen if you fall apart?" Kodi questioned.

"Kodi, I exist everywhere. I can never fall apart... even if my toy body does. I'm always here for you," Magellan said as he always did, right before he disappeared.

Kodi woke up to see that Magellan's tail had come loose and fallen off. He hugged the toy once again, as more stuffing came out.

Kodi cried because he felt like he was losing his best friend.

"I am thankful for you. I will always be thankful for you," Kodi said. Then he went into the attic and put Magellan in a box.

"You will be safe here," he said, as he tucked Magellan away.

Kodi left the attic and looked back once more at his magical friend who had taught him so much.

"I'll always love you, Magellan, and I won't forget," he said, before turning the attic light off and closing the door on his best friend.

Magellan stayed in that box for thirty years. But he never forgot Kodi, the little boy who changed his own life with just his dreams.

However, the story does not end there...

CHAPTER SIX

Kodi's story continued beyond his time with Magellan. He grew up and learned to love having two homes. He noticed how much happier his parents were now that they had their own dreams fulfilled. He made new friends, graduated from college, and eventually started a family of his own. He had a daughter named Madelyn, who was just like him. She loved to play and to dream big.

Although Kodi promised Magellan to never forget him, he did forget. At times, life felt hard. Kodi had to pay a lot of bills, he felt as if he was always rushing and never on time, and he felt overwhelmed with all of his responsibilities. Sometimes Kodi felt the same as he did when he was just a kid... all alone. He forgot the magic, he forgot Magellan, and he forgot the lessons that made up the secret recipe to getting all that his heart desired.

However, on another fateful day, all of that changed.

Kodi's mother, though very happy and fulfilled herself, was getting older. She wanted to move to a place where she could have help with everyday things that were becoming harder for her. Kodi found a great place that had round-the-clock helpers to come running whenever his mother needed help. This made both Kodi and his mother happy. But first, they had to pack up her house.

As Kodi was packing and cleaning, he remembered the attic full of things from his childhood. He pulled the ladder down and climbed into the attic. There, in the center of the room, was a dusty box. He wiped away some of the dust that was on the box and saw that it was labeled "Kodi's Things".

He smiled to himself as he began to open the box.

Kodi was surprised to see that his mother had kept all of his drawings. He pulled out one drawing at a time, and he realized something astounding: everything he had written down on those drawings had come true.

Kodi did, in fact, grow up to be a pilot. He flew planes to destinations all over the world... again and again and again. He had his own house now much like the one in his photo. It had both a pool and a tire swing, and was filled with love, friends, and family. Then Kodi noticed, at the bottom of the box, his childhood friend, Magellan. Kodi pulled him out and held the old, tattered toy up to the light.

"It's you," Kodi said as he hugged Magellan. "How could I forget about you?" Kodi looked around at all of the drawings and remembered Magellan's wise words. He knew what he had to do next.

He laid down on the dusty attic floor, hugged Magellan to his chest, and fell asleep... this time, on purpose.

Kodi dreamed that he was floating among the stars. Everywhere he looked there were planets, galaxies, and moons.

This must be the universe, he thought.

"Where am I?" Kodi asked out loud.

"You are where I live," a familiar voice boomed.

Kodi then saw Magellan, majestic and wise, walking toward him on a light beam full of stars.

"It is also where dreams live, before they become reality," Magellan stated.

"It is good to see you, old friend," Kodi said in an adult tone that Magellan was not used to.

"It's good to see you too, Kodi," Magellan replied sadly.

Sensing Magellan's sadness, Kodi began to explain. "Life is hard, Magellan. I know I promised, but I didn't always follow your advice. I forgot to believe. It was so hard to be thankful when my life became overwhelming and difficult. It was even harder to be happy for anything when bad things just kept happening. Truthfully, it was so much easier to forget you than it was to just keep hoping things would get better." Tears slipped out from Kodi's eyes.

"I never forgot you, Kodi. I gave you everything you asked for, but you stopped asking," Magellan said. Kodi realized that Magellan was right.

"Kodi, there is still time. It's never too late to create the life of your dreams," Magellan explained.

"You would still do that for me?" Kodi asked.

"I will always do it, for anyone who asks me to," Magellan said. "As I said, I'm always here for you."

Kodi hugged Magellan hard, and Magellan put his paw around Kodi's shoulder, hugging him back. After a moment, Magellan sighed. "Kodi," he said.

"Yes, old friend?" Kodi replied.

"Can I now ask you to do something for me?" Magellan questioned.

"Yes. Whatever it is, Magellan, I will do it for you," Kodi promised.

"Pay it forward, Kodi. Share my message with everyone you know," Magellan said. "I cannot help anyone if they don't know that I exist."

Kodi nodded. "I will," he said, and then he had a thought. "The old woman, the one who gave you to me. Is that what she did?"

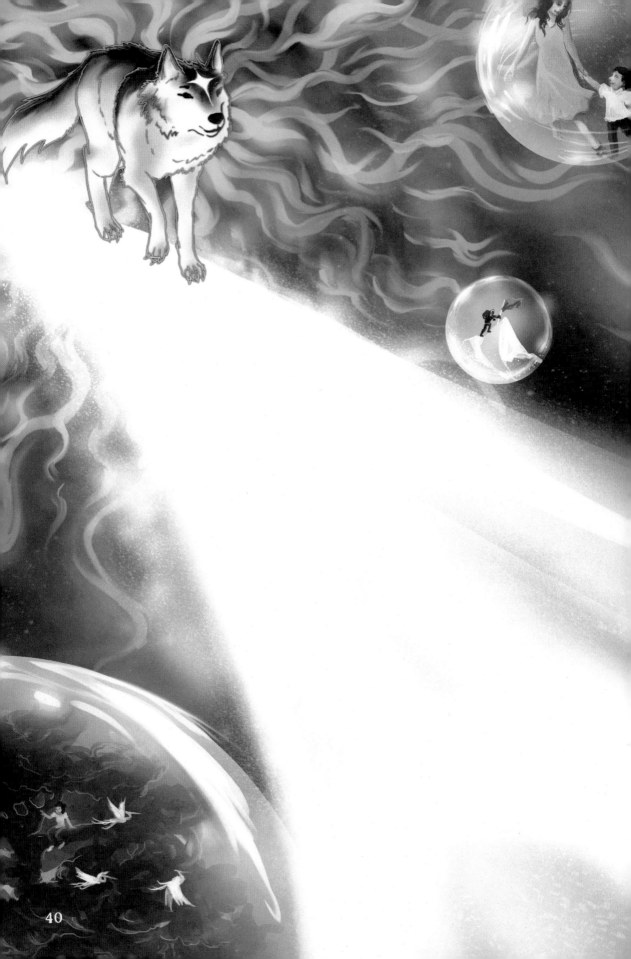

Magellan smiled and nodded, "Yes, that is my friend Tabitha. I met her when she was about the age you are now. Even as an adult, she too had a difficult time navigating the responsibilities that life piled on to her, but together we built the life of her dreams. I taught her that it's never too late to begin again. Kodi, I wanted to thank you for using your dreams to give her the apples from your tree that she loved so much. You know, Tabitha moved into your old house shortly after you drew that picture, and she enjoyed those apples for many years."

"Wow, I guess it really does work in mysterious ways," Kodi said.
"Yes, Kodi. It does."
Then they sat in silence for what seemed like an eternity. After a while, Kodi turned to Magellan, his eyes once again full of wonder, as they were when he was just a child.
"You're not really a wolf, are you?" Kodi asked.
"I am whatever you believe me to be, Kodi. I have no physical body, but I am always present. I am the Dream Weaver," he said powerfully. "But I only weave when I am commanded to by the dreams of kids like you... kids who believe and understand how powerful they are... and how powerful we can be together."
"I'm not a kid anymore, though," Kodi laughed.

"We are always like kids, no matter how old we get. As long as we believe in something beyond ourselves, we are playing, we are imagining, and we are creating, just like we did thirty years ago. I never went anywhere. You did."

Kodi nodded once again.

"You're right. I just stopped dreaming," Kodi admitted.

"Do you still remember your lessons?" Magellan asked.

"I do," Kodi responded.

"Well..." Magellan said with anticipation.

"I must write it down and say that I want it. I must believe that I will get it, and be careful with my thoughts so I don't get unkind things. I must be thankful even if I don't have it yet, and I must be happy," Kodi said, reciting his lessons from long ago.

"And?" Magellan pried.

"And... there is someone I want to introduce you to, because it's time for me to pay it forward."

"As always, lead the way," Magellan said smiling. "I'll..."

"Always be here for me. I know, and I am thankful and happy about that," Kodi interrupted, right before he woke up from his dream.

When he opened his eyes, he saw Magellan the toy wrapped in his arms. He smiled, gathered Magellan and all the drawings from the attic, and raced home.

Then Kodi did just what Magellan asked... he paid it forward.

"Madelyn, I have someone I want you to meet," Kodi said, handing Magellan to his daughter. "This is Magellan: The Magical," he said to his bright-eyed daughter. "He is a Dream Weaver."

"What makes him magical, Daddy?" she asked.

"You do, Madelyn. You do," he said, hugging his daughter gently.

Kodi never again forgot the secret recipe to making his dreams real. From that day on he lived a magical life, never forgetting to write it down, believe it, be thankful for it, and to pay it forward.

THE END

Or is it the beginning?

Now it's your turn.

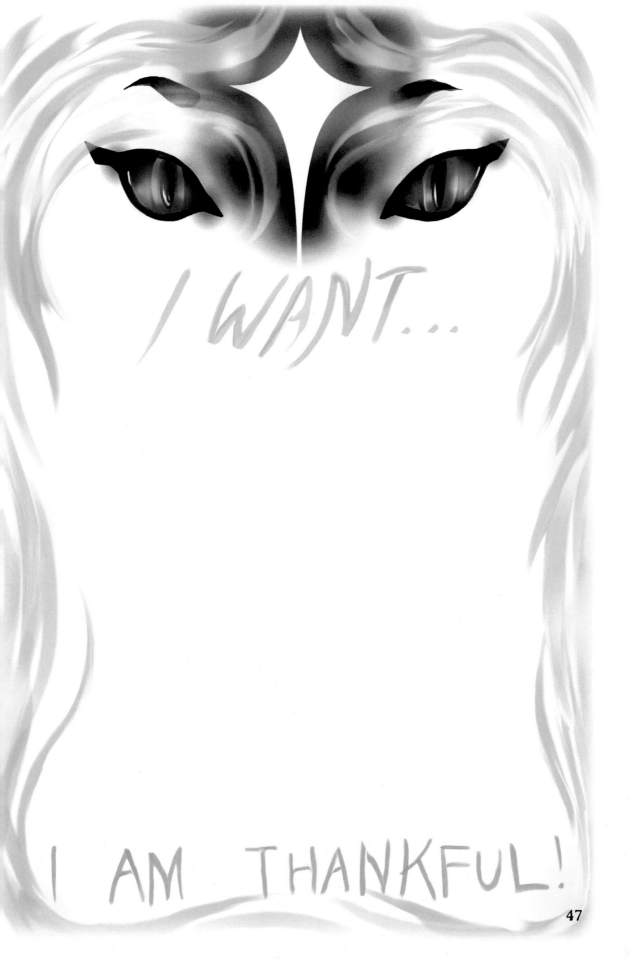